Reading Aids Series

SEMANTIC MAPPING: Classroom Applications

Joan E. Heimlich
University of Wisconsin - Whitewater

Susan D. Pittelman
University of Wisconsin - Madison

An  Service Bulletin

1986

International Reading Association
Newark, Delaware 19714

INTERNATIONAL READING ASSOCIATION

Copyright 1986 by the
International Reading Association

Library of Congress Cataloging-in-Publication Data

Heimlich, Joan E.
    Semantic mapping.

    (Reading aids series) (An IRA service bulletin)
    Bibliography: p.
    1. Reading comprehension. 2. Vocabulary—Study and teaching (Elementary) 3. Vocabulary—Study and teaching (Secondary) 4. Study, Method of. 5. English language—Semantics.
I. Pittelman, Susan D. II. Title. III. Series. IV. Series: IRA service bulletin.
LB050.45.H45   1986   371.3   86-2996
ISBN 0-87207-230-4

Contents

The research reported in this book was funded by the Wisconsin Center for Education Research which is supported in part by a grant from the National Institute of Education (Grant No. NIE-G-84-0008). The opinions expressed in this paper do not necessarily reflect the position, policy, or endorsement of the National Institute of Education.

Figures 3 to 18 were prepared by Al Divine, Wisconsin Center for Education Research, Madison, Wisconsin.

Cover by Larry Husfelt
Special thanks to Al Divine

Foreword

During the 1980s, the use of semantic mapping techniques has flourished. The term embraces a variety of strategies designed to display graphically information within categories related to a central concept. Semantic mapping is designed to help students tap their prior knowledge about a topic and expand that knowledge through vocabulary acquisition and discussion. Semantic mapping has been shown to be an effective way to learn new words, a procedure for activating students' schemata, and a technique that improves both composition and comprehension.

The present volume contains several practical classroom suggestions for the use of semantic mapping. Heimlich and Pittelman have developed an insightful and articulate synthesis of the strategy. They discuss and exemplify five applications of how semantic mapping can be used in the classroom: for general vocabulary development, as a prewriting activity, as a prereading activity, as a postreading activity, and as a study skill strategy. Their examples are taken from elementary and middle school classes in language arts, science, music, and history. Teachers who read the book will be able to generalize from the examples and discussions and transfer the applications to their own subjects and students.

Semantic Mapping: Classroom Applications is a book that will make a difference. It will become a valuable resource for teachers who are interested in the strategy. Heimlich and Pittelman are to be congratulated for writing this volume, and the International Reading Association is to be commended for contributing to the improvement of teaching through its publication.

Dale D. Johnson
Instructional Research and Development Institute
Boston, Massachusetts

vi

An Introduction to Semantic Mapping

Semantic mapping, a categorical structuring of information in graphic form, has been used successfully in a variety of classroom applications. This book provides a comprehensive introduction to this semantic based instructional strategy and presents the theoretical rationale for the effectiveness of the semantic mapping procedure as well as a review of studies. Also included are ten classroom applications of the semantic mapping procedure in a variety of content areas.

Understanding Reading Comprehension

Improving reading comprehension is a top priority as well as an area of concern for the majority of teachers today. In recent years, however, research on cognition, language acquisition, and information processing has contributed to a better understanding of the comprehension process. Much has been learned about how readers comprehend and how teachers can help improve comprehension. In light of this research, comprehension can be viewed as an active process in which readers interpret what they read in accordance with what is already known about the topic, thus building bridges between the new and the known (Pearson & Johnson, 1978).

Viewing the reading process as a mental dialogue between the writer and the reader is an outgrowth of the impact of schema theory on the research in reading comprehension. Schema theory attempts to explain how information from the text becomes integrated with the reader's prior knowledge, thus influencing the comprehension process. According to schema theorists, that which is experienced and learned is stored in the brain in networks or categories called schemata. These schemata are incomplete and are constantly being further developed. As new information is received, the schemata are restructured and fine tuned (Pearson & Spiro, 1982). For example, as a person reads about, sees pictures of, or visits a zoo, each experience adds to the schema for zoo. Each piece of new information expands and refines the existing schema.

The Role of Vocabulary in Reading Comprehension

The important role of vocabulary development in reading comprehension has been acknowledged for many years. In 1944, Davis found that word knowledge is clearly the most important factor in reading comprehension; the importance of word meanings in reading comprehension has been confirmed by current researchers as well (Barrett & Graves, 1981; Hayes & Tierney, 1982).

The increasing awareness of the influence of prior knowledge in the reading process has given even greater importance to vocabulary development. A reader's vocabulary serves as a means of labeling the ideas (or schemata) that already exist in the mind. A goal of vocabulary instruction is to develop additional labels for existing schemata, with good instruction adding to the schemata as well. Because schemata play an integral role in the comprehension process, vocabulary development is an important component of comprehension instruction.

The importance of prior knowledge and vocabulary development in reading comprehension is generally recognized by teachers and reading researchers alike. Most reading lessons, particularly those taught from a basal series, include activities for increasing background knowledge and for instruction in vocabulary development. Only recently, however, we have come to appreciate fully the critical role that a student's prior knowledge plays in reading comprehension.

Comprehension, no longer viewed as simply getting meaning from the printed page, is seen as an active process in which students integrate prior knowledge with text information to create new knowledge (Adams & Bruce, 1980). Skilled readers actively call into play and integrate the knowledge and experiences stored in their memories with the words on the printed page (Durkin, 1981). In fact, research has shown that background knowledge about a topic, particularly understanding of key vocabulary, is a better predictor of text comprehension than is any measure of reading ability or achievement (Johnston & Pearson, 1982; Johnston, 1984).

To maximize reading comprehension, teachers need to find ways to help students activate and retrieve prior knowledge related to the topic about which they will be reading (National Institute of Education, 1978). They must provide activities that give students an opportunity to mobilize existing information (schemata) so that readers are ready to relate to their reading. Similarly, vocabulary must be introduced in a meaningful way so that existing knowledge is activated, allowing the new information to be linked to the old. For vocabulary instruction to be effective, however, the instruction must not be limited to individual word meanings, but rather attention must be given to the schemata or entire conceptual framework elicited by the word meaning. Recent vocabulary research has confirmed the advantage of a concept development approach to vocabulary instruction over the more conventional definition and sentence approach. In concept development approaches, the emphasis is on where a word fits in a reader's semantic repertoire, rather than being limited to what the word means or how it is used in sentences (Pearson, 1985).

The Instructional Strategy of Semantic Mapping

Recently, both teachers and researchers have given attention to the instructional strategy of semantic mapping. Semantic mapping is a method that activates and builds on a student's prior knowledge base. This strategy provides an alternative to traditional prereading and vocabulary building activities typically included in basal reading series.

Semantic mapping is not new; it has been around for years under the labels "semantic webbing," "semantic networking," or "plot maps." The value of semantic mapping, however, has only recently been recognized due to an increased understanding of the important role that prior knowledge plays in the reading process. The semantic mapping process influences students to become active readers by triggering the brain to retrieve what is known about the topic and to use this information in reading. This activation of prior knowledge is critical to reading comprehension.

Semantic maps are diagrams that help students see how words are related to one another. While the semantic mapping procedure may vary according to individual teacher objectives, the procedure generally includes a brainstorming session in which students are asked to verbalize associations to the topic or stimulus words as the teacher maps (categorizes) them on the chalkboard. This phase of semantic mapping provides students with an opportunity to engage actively in a mental activity which retrieves stored prior knowledge and to see graphically the concepts they are retrieving. Students learn the meanings and uses of new words, see old words in a new light, and see the relationships among words. Through discussion, the students can verify and expand their own understandings of the concepts. They relate new concepts to their own background knowledge, thus promoting better comprehension.

The Effectiveness of Semantic Mapping

Studies to evaluate the effectiveness of semantic mapping have supported the use of semantic mapping as an effective teaching strategy. Toms-Bronowski (1983) found that fourth through sixth grade children who were taught target vocabulary words through semantic mapping and semantic feature analysis significantly outperformed students who learned the words through contextual analysis. Analysis of retention test scores also indicated that the two prior knowledge strategies were more effective than contextual analysis (Johnson, Toms-Bronowski, & Pittelman, 1982). Margosein, Pascarella, and Pflaum (1982) found that semantic mapping had a greater impact on vocabulary acquisition than did the context cue approach for reading disabled seventh and eighth graders of Hispanic background.

Karbon (1984) conducted a study with rural Native American, innercity Black, and suburban sixth graders to examine the resources and processes used by children of different cultural groups during vocabulary instruction. Karbon found that students do exploit their unique experiences as a means of developing vocabulary. She recommends that teachers use vocabulary techniques that build on prior knowledge, emphasizing that semantic mapping provides an alternative technique to vocabulary instruction that focuses on the relationships between new and known words.

Pittelman, Levin, and Johnson (1985) studied poor readers to see whether they learn more from semantic mapping vocabulary instruction when they are taught with other poor readers in a small group or when they receive whole class instruction with students of mixed reading abilities. Group size did not matter. Furthermore, poor readers who received semantic mapping instruction had significantly higher gain scores than did students in control classes. The study confirmed that teachers can feel comfortable using semantic mapping in both reading ability groups and whole class content area instruction.

Results from studies evaluating the use of semantic mapping as a prereading strategy have also supported the effectiveness of the semantic mapping procedure. In a study of fourth and fifth graders, Hagen (1980) found that semantic mapping was not only an effective motivator, but also served as a valuable diagnostic tool for assessing a student's prior knowledge and encouraged divergent thinking.

Johnson, Pittelman, Toms-Bronowski, and Levin (1984) compared semantic mapping with semantic feature analysis and a basal approach for effectiveness as prereading instructional treatments for both vocabulary acquisition and passage comprehension with fourth grade students. All three prereading treatments were effective in teaching target vocabulary words. Both semantic mapping and semantic feature analysis had a facilitative effect on passage comprehension. Jones (1984) replicated a portion of that study with Black innercity fifth graders. She concluded that semantic mapping does positively affect vocabulary acquisition and passage specific comprehension of expository passages.

Recent research, then, has confirmed the effectiveness of using the semantic based strategy of semantic mapping in vocabulary and comprehension instruction.

Semantic Mapping As an Instructional Strategy

Three of the most commonly used applications of the semantic mapping strategy are 1) for general vocabulary development, 2) for pre and postreading, and 3) as a study skill technique. A description is presented of each of these three applications of the semantic mapping procedure.

Semantic Mapping in Vocabulary Development

Perhaps the most widely known use of semantic mapping as an instructional strategy in general vocabulary development is the one suggested by Johnson and Pearson (1984). Their application of semantic mapping as a strategy to enhance comprehension is a logical one, since it draws heavily on activating prior knowledge of the topic. This semantic mapping procedure prepares students to understand, assimilate, and evaluate the information to be read. It also capitalizes on the use of word knowledge which has been shown to be the most important factor in reading comprehension (Davis, 1944; Spearritt, 1972; Thorndike, 1971). Following is an adaptation of the Johnson and Pearson procedure (1984, pp. 12-13).

1. Choose a word or topic related to classroom work.
2. List the word on a large chart tablet or on the chalkboard.
3. Encourage the students to think of as many words as they can that are related to the selected key word and then to list the words by categories on a sheet of paper.
4. Students then share the prepared lists orally and all words are written on the class map in categories.
5. The joint effort of the class might resemble Figure 1, a map developed by a fourth grade class for the topic *Stores*.
6. Students can gain further practice in classification by labeling the categories on the semantic map.
   a. People
   b. Kinds
   c. Problems
   d. Expenses of owning
   e. Prices

7. Discussion of the semantic map is, perhaps, the most important part of the lesson. The purpose of the exercise is to encourage students to become aware of new words, to gather new meanings from old words, and to see the relationships among all the words.

Semantic Mapping in Pre and Postreading

The basic semantic mapping vocabulary building technique developed by Johnson and Pearson has also been used in pre and postreading situations. In addition to being effective for vocabulary development, semantic mapping has been demonstrated to be a good alternative to traditional activities used before reading a new passage, as well as after reading a passage. In this application, semantic mapping not only can be used to introduce the key vocabulary words from the passage to be read but can provide the teacher with an assessment of the students' prior knowledge, or schema availability, on the topic. The semantic mapping procedure activates the students' prior knowledge of the topic, helping them to focus on relevant schema and thereby better preparing them to understand, assimilate, and evaluate the information in the material to be read. After reading the selection, a discussion of the semantic map can be refocused to emphasize the main ideas presented in the written material.

In this application, students develop a map of the story's topic before reading both to learn the key vocabulary necessary for comprehension and to activate their prior knowledge bases of that topic. The semantic mapping exercise also motivates students to read the selection and provides the teacher with an assessment tool.

As the story is read, or after reading the story, students can add words and new categories to their own copies of the map. In the final phase of the semantic mapping procedure, which is a class discussion, there is an opportunity for the identification and integration of the new information. This class discussion can also serve as a comprehension check for the teacher.

Semantic mapping as a pre and postreading strategy is effective with basal as well as with other reading materials and has been successfully adapted to content instruction as well. As a postreading activity, semantic mapping affords students the opportunity to recall, organize, and represent graphically the pertinent information read.

Semantic Mapping As a Study Skill Strategy

Hanf (1971) elaborated on the semantic mapping strategy, using it as a study skill to guide the processing of textbook material. She suggested that semantic mapping be used as an advance organizer, enabling better comprehension, as well as an effective substitute for the traditional notetaking and outlining procedure. In Hanf's procedure, mapping is used as a study skill technique with either individuals or groups.

Figure 1
Classroom Map for *Stores*

Hanf suggested that students use three basic steps to design a map of content information from a text.

1. *Identification of main idea.* The title or main idea is written on a sheet of paper and a shape is drawn around it. Students then think of all they already know about the topic and decide what they expect to find in the chapter. Next, students write three or four questions about the topic on the other side of the map.

2. *Secondary categories.* The principal parts of the textbook chapter will form the secondary categories in the semantic map. Before reading the textbook, students hypothesize what the basic parts of the chapter will be and then skim the chapter for the accuracy of their hypotheses. Labels for the secondary categories are then written on the map. (If sections in the text have not been labeled, the secondary categories must be summarized and labeled.) Hanf suggested that no more than six or seven secondary categories be used on one map and that a category of evaluation, in which the reader judges and assesses the quality of the material, always be included. The secondary categories organized around the main idea complete the structure of the map and provide "a picture of the intellectual territory" to explore and conquer. Hanf recommended that students place a question mark after each category label so they know what information to be reading for.

3. *Supporting details.* In this final step of the procedure, students read the chapter for details and complete the map by adding the details from memory. Hanf pointed out that the value in adding the details to the map from memory is that students are immediately held accountable for knowing the facts for each secondary category. The map provides immediate feedback about whether students need to reread the chapter to add more information to any of the categories. The completed map provides a graphic summary of the information in the chapter. A completed study map for the topic *Black Widow Spiders* is presented in Figure 2.

Hanf uses semantic mapping as a study technique. Like the Johnson and Pearson technique, it is useful in both reading and content areas. The Hanf technique, however, is primarily used in the content areas.

Figure 2
Study Map for *Black Widow Spiders*

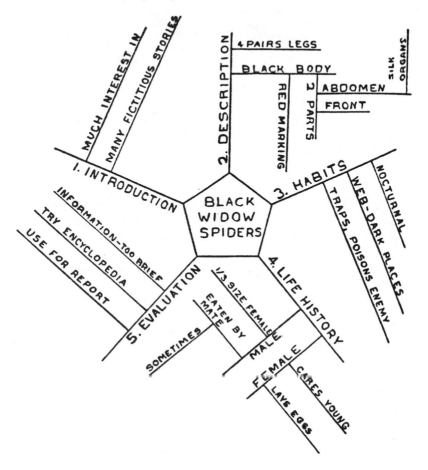

From M. Buckley Hanf, "Mapping: A Technique for Translating Reading into Thinking," *Journal of Reading*, January 1971, p. 228.

Classroom Applications of Semantic Mapping

Three basic applications of semantic mapping were described previously: the Johnson and Pearson vocabulary building strategy, the Johnson and Pearson prereading strategy, and the Hanf study technique. Using these three basic procedures as models, teachers have modified and adapted semantic mapping to meet their specific lesson and unit objectives.

In this chapter, ten specific applications of the semantic mapping procedure in elementary and middleschool classrooms are presented. These examples were selected to demonstrate the usability and adaptability of the semantic mapping procedure. Students participating in the lessons ranged from first through eighth grade; most lessons were developed for whole classes although small group and individual applications are also included. The lesson plans are based on written documentation as well as on teacher interviews. At the end of each lesson are comments which highlight the unique contributions of the semantic mapping procedure. Reproductions of the classroom semantic maps are provided for each lesson.

A Guided Postreading Activity: Grade One

In this application, semantic mapping is used with six first graders reading at a primer level. The students read a story from a basal series and then participate in a semantic mapping activity to reinforce the story vocabulary and to build comprehension skills and preliminary outlining skills. (See Figure 3.)

Objectives

The semantic mapping process is used to meet the following objectives:
- Reinforce the new vocabulary in the story.
- Recall and locate information from a story.

Figure 3
Classroom Map for *Kate and the Zoo*

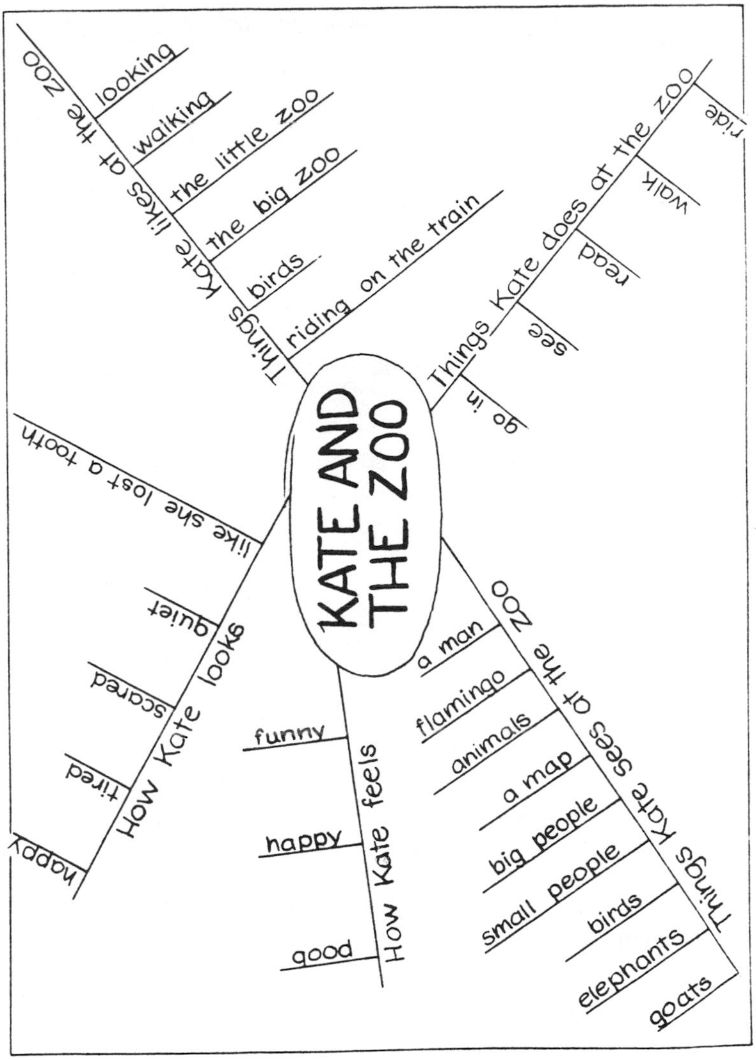

KATE AND THE ZOO

Things Kate likes at the zoo
- looking
- walking
- the little zoo
- the big zoo
- birds
- riding on the train

Things Kate does at the zoo
- go in
- see
- read
- walk
- ride

like she lost a tooth

How Kate looks
- quiet
- scared
- tired
- happy

How Kate feels
- funny
- happy
- good

Things Kate sees at the zoo
- a man
- flamingo
- animals
- a map
- big people
- small people
- birds
- elephants
- goats

- Organize information from a story by topic.
- Infer meaning from pictures and printed information.

Procedure

Day 1

1. Tell the students that they are going to read a story about a little girl, Kate, who goes to the zoo. Introduce the key vocabulary words as suggested in the teacher's manual.
2. Using the procedure suggested in the teacher's manual, have the students read the story.
3. Explain to the students that they are going to be making a special kind of map and that this map will contain the important information from the story.
4. Print the title of the story, *Kate and the Zoo,* on the chalkboard and draw a circle around it.
5. Print topic headings on the map that will draw on both literal and inferential information presented through the text and the pictures in the story, i.e. "Things Kate sees at the zoo," "Things Kate does at the zoo," and "Things Kate likes at the zoo" (literal); "How Kate looks," "How Kate feels" (inferential).
6. Ask students to share information they remember from the story. After a student has responded, have that student decide under which topic heading the information should be written. Then add the information to the map.
7. Have other students suggest additional information from the story that could fit under this same topic heading.
8. After several students have had the opportunity to add information under the first heading, select another topic heading and ask students to recall information from the story that would belong under this heading.
9. Continue with the procedure until students have had an opportunity to contribute information under all the topic headings on the map.

Day 2

1. Review the map for *Kate and the Zoo.*
2. Explain to the students that they are going to reread the story to look for any information that is in the story but has not been written on the map.
3. Guide the reading of the story page by page. As students find new information, have them share it with the group. Then let the students decide under which heading the information belongs. Print that information under the appropriate topic heading.

4. Duplicate the completed map and give each student a copy to take home. Encourage them to use their copy of the map to help retell the story to their parents.

Comments

This example illustrates how semantic mapping can be used as part of a reading lesson with first graders reading at a primer level. Because the students were inexperienced with semantic mapping and story structure, the teacher suggested the topic headings and elicited information by topic rather than using the more common brainstorming technique. (In brainstorming, information is listed as it is suggested and is not limited by topic or category. Information is then categorized, or mapped, through group discussion.)

The semantic mapping activities encouraged these first graders to draw upon and apply information they had read. In adding information under the literal topic headings on the map, students used information taken directly from the text. Adding information under the inferential topic headings, however, required students to move beyond the written word, to relate what they saw in the pictures and read in the story to their own experiences, thereby promoting active participation in the reading process.

The graphic structure of the semantic map helped the students organize the information gained through reading. This experience, in general, develops preliminary organizational skills that students will build on as they become more fluent readers and writers.

A Pre and Postreading Vocabulary Building and Writing Activity: Grade One

In this application, semantic mapping is used with fifteen first graders near the end of the school year. Students read a story in their basal series that relates to a science topic being studied and then organize the information from the story onto a semantic map. The students use the map to help them write a short report of several sentences. Mapping is done prior to and after students read the passage and again after students have done independent reading from resource books and viewed a filmstrip. Students, who have been studying wildlife creatures, research the topic *Sea Otters* and write reports for their wildlife folders. (See Figures 4 and 5.)

Objectives

The semantic mapping process is used to meet the following objectives:

- Assess students' knowledge of sea otters.
- Share prior knowledge of sea otters with peers.
- Learn new vocabulary related to sea otters.
- Organize and structure the information about sea otters.

Figure 4
Initial Classroom Map for *Sea Otters*

Figure 5
Completed Classroom Map for *Sea Otters*

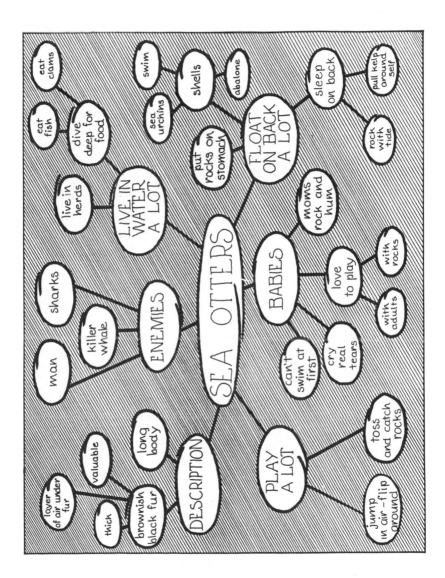

Procedure

Day 1

1. Place a picture of sea otters on the chalkboard. Then print the words *Sea Otters* below the picture and draw a circle around the words.
2. Ask the students to think about sea otters and to share as many words as they can that relate to the topic.
3. Discuss and record on the map information and words that the students suggest. Write this information on the chalkboard in clusters (categories) using white chalk.
4. As necessary, add and define key vocabulary words important to story comprehension (words that had been suggested by the basal series). Write these words on the map with blue chalk.
5. Discuss each of the clusters or categories of words and determine appropriate labels or headings. Add these to the map.
6. Have the students read the story by following the procedure suggested in the teacher's manual.
7. After the students have finished reading the story, ask them to suggest new information that can be added to the map. Write this information on the map using green chalk. (See Figure 4.)

Day 2

1. Review the information about sea otters on the semantic map. Ask the students what else they would like to know about sea otters.
2. Give the students resource books to read for additional information about sea otters. Have the students write down important information they learn from reading these books.
3. Have the students use their notes during a discussion period in which they share the information about sea otters gained through their independent reading. Add new information to the map using red chalk.

Day 3

1. Briefly review the categories on the semantic map.
2. Tell the students that you are going to show them a filmstrip about sea otters and they should look for information to add to the categories on the semantic map.
3. Show the filmstrip.
4. Discuss the information from the filmstrip. Add this new information to the map using yellow chalk. (See Figure 5.)
5. Direct each student to select three to five facts about sea otters from the map. Have students use these facts to write complete sentences. These will form their reports about the sea otter.
6. Have the students illustrate their reports.
7. Let each student read his or her completed report and share the accompanying illustration with the entire class. Place these reports in the students' wildlife folders.

Comments

This activity illustrates how semantic mapping can be used in the primary grades to integrate science, reading, and writing. Using a picture above the written topic label is an effective technique for use with primary students as it stimulates the children's thoughts and gets the brainstorming procedure off to a quick start. The mapping experience was not only motivational but it also gave the first graders the opportunity to share new and known vocabulary, to read for new facts and ideas, and to see how information can be organized. The completed map helped them with their report writing by serving as a guide in information selection, as a springboard for ideas, and as a spelling guide for writing their sentences.

The map itself provided the students with a graphic picture of the "territory they had traveled," showing what they already knew, prior knowledge (written in white chalk); what they learned in reading their basal text (green chalk); what they learned from their independent reading (red chalk); and the information from viewing the filmstrip (yellow chalk). At each stage of the map's development, students could refine as well as add to the existing map. While the maps reproduced here in black and white do not show the effect of the use of different colors of chalk, the additions to the map can be seen by comparing the initial map (Figure 4) with the completed map (Figure 5).

A Prereading and Vocabulary Building Activity: Grade Two

In this application, semantic mapping is used with fifteen high average second grade students preparing to read a story in their basal readers about Washington, D.C. The teacher combines the use of a basal story and a large poster map to organize and study the topic. (See Figure 6.)

Objectives

A modified Hanf semantic mapping process is used to meet the following objectives:
- Introduce key vocabulary words prior to reading a basal passage.
- Share prior knowledge about Washington, D.C.
- Learn about Washington, D.C. using more than one source.
- Organize new information and vocabulary into a graphic form.
- Recall and use information from the map for oral discussion.

Procedure

1. Tape a poster of a Washington, D.C. map on one side of the chalkboard. Tell the students they are going to be reading a story about Washington, D.C.

Figure 6
Completed Classroom Map for *Washington, D.C.*

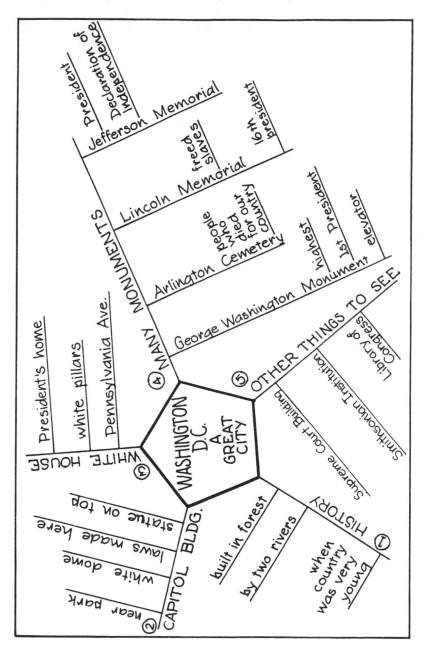

2. Write the words "Washington, D.C. – A Great City" in the middle of the chalkboard and draw a circle around the words.
3. Introduce the key vocabulary words from the basal passage by writing sentences about Washington on the chalkboard.
4. Have the students skim the passage in the basal text to find the subtopics printed in italics. Discuss each subtopic as you write it in white chalk on the map as a category heading. (Several of the key vocabulary words appear in the subtopic titles.)
5. Give students an opportunity to share information they already know about these subtopics and add this information to the map in red chalk under the appropriate category heading. Explain to the students that you are using red chalk to indicate what information they knew about Washington before they read the story.
6. Have the students read the passage, stopping at the end of each subtopic to discuss the information they have learned about Washington. As students share facts they have learned, write them on the chalkboard map under the proper heading. Point out that you are using white chalk to indicate what information on their map they learned from reading the story.
7. Discuss the information presented in the poster as it relates to the headings on the map. Using blue chalk, add any new information from the poster, including historical places and descriptions, to the chalkboard map. Explain that you are using blue chalk so they will be able to tell which information on the map they learned from the poster.
8. Using the completed semantic map, help the students to summarize information learned about Washington, D.C. (A copy of the map is shown in Figure 6.)

Comments

In this lesson, semantic mapping meets a variety of objectives. First, it was a prereading activity to prepare students to read a basal passage. Then the map was used to guide the actual reading of the passage. Information about the topic from the passage was added to the map during the reading. The map was also used to help students synthesize the information presented on the poster. The poster served as a foundation around which students could visually organize new information. Finally, the map was used as a tool to help students summarize and retell the information.

The use of semantic mapping in a prereading lesson is quite common and is, indeed, an effective strategy. Participation in a semantic mapping experience not only activates students' prior knowledge regarding the topic, but also provides an effective way to reinforce key vocabulary words, allowing students to incorporate the new vocabulary into their existing schemata.

The use of colored chalk helps students recognize that the information came from a variety of sources, including the poster and their reading of the basal story. These two sources, when added to the students' own prior knowledge, helped to form a more complete picture of Washington, D.C. The success of this experience reinforces the value of using several sources of information to study a topic.

A Study Skill Strategy in Science: Grade Five

In this application, a modification of the Hanf semantic mapping technique is used to help twenty-five fifth grade students prepare for an exam on the digestive system. In an extensive unit on the digestive system, a variety of instructional materials and activities was used, including textbooks, filmstrips, take-a-part models of the human body, actual digestive organs of several animals, X-rays, posters, transparencies and a lecture by a local physician. The mapping strategy will help these students organize all the information presented in the unit and serve as a review technique to study for a test. (See Figure 7.)

Objectives

An adaptation of the Hanf semantic mapping process is used to meet the following objectives:
- Select important information from the unit of study.
- Organize the information onto a semantic map.
- Learn technical information and vocabulary about the digestive system.
- Develop a study guide.

Procedure

1. Tell the students they are going to use a new type of review procedure called mapping to assist them as they study for their unit test on the digestive system. Then write the word *Digestion* on the chalkboard and explain the procedure of semantic mapping.
2. Tell the students to write the word *digestion* in the center of their own papers and draw lines radiating out from the center.
3. Direct the students to skim the chapter on digestion in their textbooks to identify the secondary category headings.
4. Have the students write on the lines of their maps the secondary category headings from the chapter.
5. Tell the students to close their books. Then ask the students to work independently to recall details or facts from the book about each of the categories and add them to their own maps.

Figure 7
Completed Classroom Map for *Digestion*

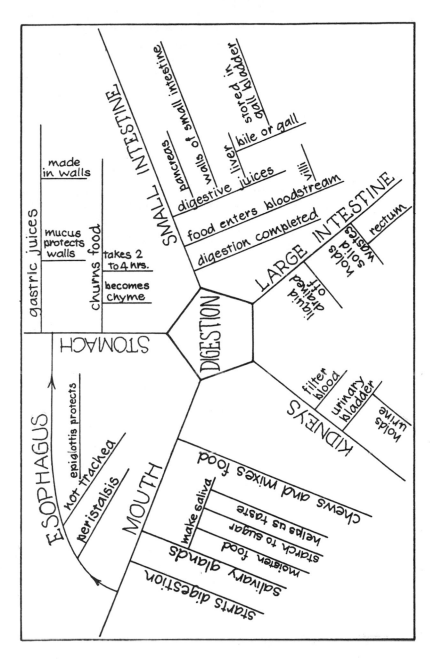

6. After the students have completed their individual recall maps, have them develop a group map on the chalkboard, share details from their individual maps, and discuss them. Add new information to the appropriate category on the group map. Encourage the students to add new information to their individual maps.

7. Upon completion of the group recall map, direct the students to re-read their textbooks to locate additional pertinent information for each of the secondary categories. Tell the students that as they find new information they should add it to their individual maps.

8. Through group discussion, students share the additional information obtained through the textbook review. Add this information to the group map, emphasizing technical vocabulary words. The students then update their individual maps.

9. Ask the students to survey their individual maps and think about the various activities they experienced in the unit. Ask them to share any other information they feel is important to understanding the digestive system. Add this information to the group map and have the students add it to their individual maps. (The completed group map is shown in Figure 7.)

10. Encourage students to use their maps to study for the unit test. They may find the map to be a helpful study tool whether they choose to study individually, in pairs, in small groups, or with parents and siblings.

Comments

In this example, semantic mapping was used to summarize unit information and served as a study technique at the end of the unit, rather than as a guide to unit development. The mapping procedure assisted students in drawing together and organizing the large amount of information presented throughout the unit. To create the map, students had to understand the relationship between the major topic, its subcategories, and the supporting details. The teacher reported that the students experienced difficulty with the placement of the term *esophagus* on the map. They didn't feel the term fit either the category "stomach" or the category "mouth" and settled upon a curved line connecting the two categories.

The completed map became a one page, quick and easy way of reviewing for the unit test. Students then had several studying options as they prepared for the unit test; they could use the map to study alone, in pairs, or in small groups.

Here semantic mapping was used with a heterogeneous group. Not only did the procedure meet the teacher's specified objectives of organizing information and preparing students for a test, but it also served to provide a positive learning experience for these students. The mapping activity also introduced the students to an individual study procedure useful for organizing information from content area material or outlines of lectures and class discussions. Another benefit of this approach is that students learn to feel comfortable about participating in classroom discussions. The teacher reported that regardless of ability, each student was able to make a worthwhile contribution to the map.

Semantic Mapping in Music: Grades Two through Five

In this application, semantic mapping is used to review vocabulary words and symbols related to music. This approach is used over an extended period of time with classes of students in grades two through five. The vocabulary words and musical symbols included on the maps varied according to the grade level of the students. The map provided shows the results of this activity with a third grade class. (See Figures 8 and 9.)

Objectives

The semantic mapping process is used to meet the following objectives:
- Assess the students' knowledge of music.
- Identify the five components of music.
- Transcribe vocabulary words into musical symbols.
- Review the five components of music.

Procedure

Day 1
1. Write the word *Music* on the chalkboard. Then draw a box around the word.
2. Ask the students to think about the topic *music* and to suggest as many words as they can which relate to the concept. As words are suggested, list them on the chalkboard.
3. After the class is over, group the appropriate words the students provided under the five components of music: melody, rhythm, harmony, expression, and form. Copy the map onto a transparency overlay using a blue marking pen. (The third grade version of the initial map is shown in Figure 8.)

Day 2
1. Using an overhead projector, show the transparency overlay of the map to the students.
2. Introduce the five components of music, pointing to each component on the map. Tell the students that you wrote some of the words they

Figure 8
Initial Classroom Map for *Music*

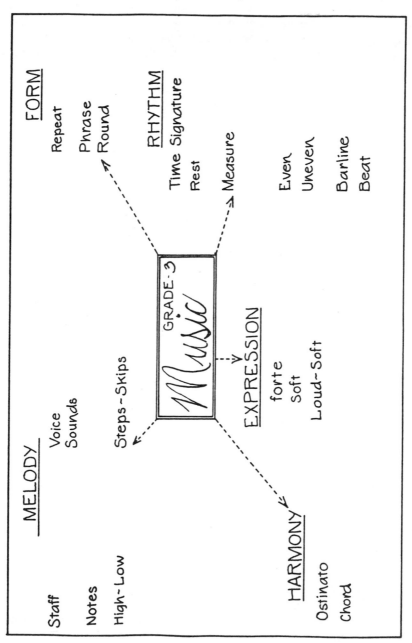

Figure 9
Completed Classroom Map for *Music*

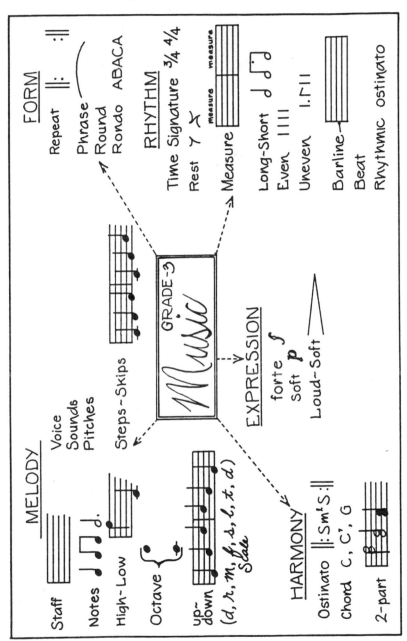

had suggested the previous day under the appropriate component of music.

3. Review each of the five components of music and the words written under each component.

4. Give the students an opportunity to look through their music textbooks to find more words that relate to each of the five components of music. Add these words to the map using a red marking pen.

Succeeding Days

1. Have the students continue to use their textbooks to find additional words to write on the map. As they suggest words, add them to the map using a red pen.

2. After the students have completed their textbook search, review the words the students knew prior to their textbook searches (words in blue) as well as words they added to the map as a result of their textbook search (words in red).

3. Explain that music has a unique vocabulary that can be almost totally translated into musical symbols. Next lay a blank transparency over the transparency of the original vocabulary map.

4. Read each word on the map and, whenever appropriate, transcribe that word into a musical symbol. Write each musical symbol on the blank transparency next to its English word.

5. After class, transfer the information from the two maps onto a single sheet of paper. This completed map will contain the five components of music and its vocabulary with the corresponding symbols. The completed maps will differ in complexity according to grade level. (The completed third grade map is shown in Figure 9.) Give each student a copy of the map to take home and encourage the students to share the map with their families.

Comments

It is gratifying to see semantic mapping—an approach that has been used primarily in language arts, science, and social studies—successfully applied to the creative arts. As demonstrated in this lesson, mapping is an effective way to introduce musical concepts. The procedure draws out what individual students already know and then expands on the concepts through sharing of students' ideas.

This semantic mapping activity produced a graphic picture of the relationship among the five components of music, as well as the relationship of the vocabulary within each component. Adding musical symbols to the map provided a meaningful transition from the written vocabulary to the symbolic representation of the words.

There is great potential for using mapping to teach musical content, including families of instruments, periods of music, and various types of ethnic music. The semantic mapping technique is a beneficial tool that provides a framework for students to organize newly introduced information.

A Pre and Postreading Vocabulary Building Activity: Grade Six

In this application, semantic mapping is used with twelve poor readers in a sixth grade remedial reading class over a period of several days. The students are preparing to read a story about rattlesnakes. They participate in semantic mapping pre and postreading activities designed to develop vocabulary and to enhance comprehension. (See Figure 10.)

Objectives

The semantic mapping process is used to meet the following objectives:
- Assess students' background of experiences related to rattlesnakes.
- Retrieve known vocabulary related to the central topic, *Rattlesnakes*.
- Connect new concepts (vocabulary) to known information through discussion.
- Organize information into categories.
- Generate research questions about the topic.

Procedure

Day 1
1. Write the word *rattlesnakes* on the chalkboard and draw a circle around the word.
2. Ask the students to think of words or ideas related to the topic, *Rattlesnakes*.
3. List the words the students suggest on the chalkboard. (A sample copy of the students' word list is presented in Figure 11.)
4. Discuss the words in the list. Next, write these words on the semantic map, placing them in clusters or categories. After further discussion, have the students label each category on the map.
5. Through discussion, students formulate research questions about hunting rattlesnakes (i.e., "Why would people hunt rattlesnakes?" and "How do people hunt rattlesnakes?"). Write these questions on the chalkboard.
6. Direct the students to read the story, "Rattlesnake Hunt" and to find the answers to as many questions as possible. Tell the students to also look for other new information about rattlesnakes to add to the semantic map.

Figure 10
Group Map for *Rattlesnakes*

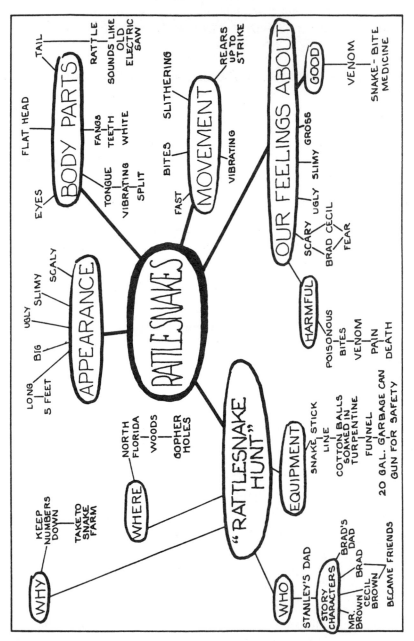

Figure 11
Student Elicited Word List for *Rattlesnakes*

gross	*fangs	pain
long	vibrating	ugly
tongue	slimy	big
* rattle	scaly	Stanley (dad
tail	scary	catches snakes)
fast	poisonous	hunt
slithering	* venom	harmful
teeth	* bites	death

*Indicates new vocabulary from story
The words are presented in the order the students suggested them.

7. After the students have finished reading the story, discuss the answers to the questions formulated about rattlesnake hunting. Add new information about rattlesnakes to the map as it is suggested. As information related to the structure of the story (plot and characters) is contributed, add it to the classroom map as well.

8. After the students have had an opportunity to add all of the new information to the map, have them make their own copies of the semantic map from the chalkboard.

Day 2

1. Through discussion, review the information on the semantic map that is specific to story structure as well as to rattlesnakes in general. Then have the students pose additional research questions not answered by the information on the map (i.e., "How is venom made into medicine?" "How does snakebite medicine work to keep people from dying?" and "What are snake farms?").

2. Give the students the opportunity to do research to answer the questions generated.

3. Tell the students that as they do their own research, they should add the new information to their individual maps.

29

Day 3

1. Have students share the results of their research through a class discussion. As new information is shared, add it to the classroom map. The product of the group mapping is shown in Figure 10.

Comments

The use of semantic mapping in this lesson was unique in that the mapping activities focused on story structure as well as on information related to rattlesnakes.

Before reading the story the students participated in an activity in which vocabulary words related to rattlesnakes were elicited from the students. (See Figure 11.) The teacher felt that writing the words on the chalkboard instead of directly on the map allowed students the opportunity to study the list before having to organize the words into categories. This vocabulary also prepared students for reading by having students retrieve known information (vocabulary) related to the topic.

After the initial map had been developed, the teacher and students studied the map and formulated questions about the topic. Formulating questions involved students in using the related vocabulary words on the map and prompted them to become personally and actively involved as they thought about and determined what they wanted to know about the topic.

The class discussion after story reading involved both answering the formulated questions and adding new information to the map. During this session the unexpected occurred—students found that they still had unanswered questions, thus prompting them to engage in further research and additional mapping.

The teacher found that the mapping process also enabled her to illustrate graphically and to reinforce story structure including plot, characters, and main ideas. The mapping of information related to story structure offers teachers an additional technique for evaluating whether students have understood a story.

A Pre and Postreading Vocabulary Building Activity: Grade Eight

In this application, semantic mapping is used as a pre and postreading vocabulary building strategy with two eighth grade remedial reading classes, each having twelve students. Students use mapping (over a period of three lessons) both prior to and after reading a basal story and again after independent research has been done on the topic. (See Figures 12 and 13.)

Objectives

The semantic mapping process is used to meet the following objectives:
- Assess students' prior knowledge of sharks.
- Learn key vocabulary words.
- Share prior knowledge and known vocabulary.
- Read and comprehend the story.
- Gain additional information about sharks.
- Reinforce the skill of using reference materials.

Procedure

Day 1

1. Write the word *Sharks* on an overhead transparency with a black marker and draw a circle around the word.
2. Ask the students to think of as many words and ideas as they can that relate to the word *sharks*.
3. Using the black marker, list on the map in clusters or categories the words that students volunteer.
4. Have the students suggest labels for the categories and write them on the map.
5. If there are any key vocabulary words important to the comprehension of the story that have not been mentioned by the students, mention them and add them to the map with a red marker. (A copy of the map is shown in Figure 12.)
6. Direct students to read the story by following the procedure suggested in the teacher's manual.
7. After students have finished reading the story, ask them to share the information they have learned about sharks. (This discussion will help you to assess story comprehension.) Add new information about sharks to the map using a green marker.

Day 2

1. Using the semantic map, review the information about sharks on the map.
2. Ask students what other information they would like to know about sharks and formulate research questions.
3. Have the students do research in the school library to answer these questions.

Day 3

1. Have students discuss and share the information acquired from their independent research.
2. During discussion, add the new information in blue ink to the appropriate category on the map. (The completed map is shown in Figure 13.)

Figure 12
Initial Classroom Map for *Sharks*

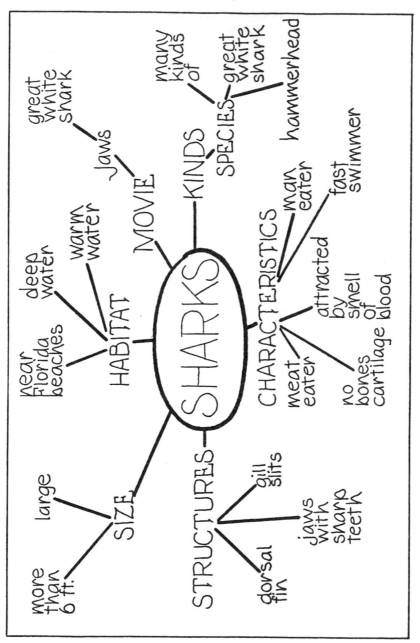

Figure 13
Completed Classroom Map for *Sharks*

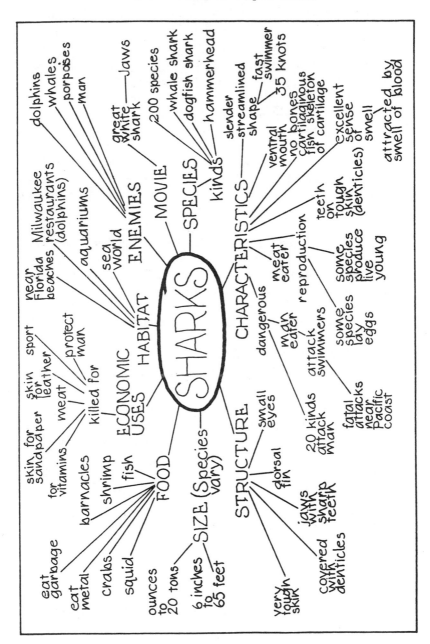

3. Using the color coded map, help students distinguish among prior knowledge, newly acquired information, and technical vocabulary used to understand the topic *Sharks*.

Comments

A strength of semantic mapping is that it allows students to share information from their own prior knowledge. The teacher of this lesson reported that an idea or fact from one student seemed to trigger ideas from other students in a chain reaction thought process.

An overhead projector and colored marking pens were used in this lesson to differentiate information from four sources: 1) information elicited from the students, 2) vocabulary (key words) contributed by the teacher, 3) information obtained through the students' reading of the story, and 4) information derived from the students' research. The color coding emphasized students' prior knowledge and the vast amount of newly acquired information.

Figure 12 depicts students' prior knowledge regarding sharks, while Figure 13 shows the completed map. Using information from reading the basal passage and from their independent research, these students were able to identify and correct misinformation written on the original map. From the second map it is evident how much additional information the students learned about the topic through reading, discussion, and research.

A Prewriting Organizer: Grade Six

In this application, semantic mapping is combined with the language experience approach. It is used individually with sixth graders to help them develop their writing skills. These students are enrolled in a remedial language arts program because they are experiencing difficulty in reading comprehension and in writing basic paragraphs. (See Figures 14 and 15.)

Objectives

The semantic mapping process is used to meet the following objectives:
- Identify information regarding a topic of interest.
- Identify main ideas and supporting details of the topic.
- Organize prior knowledge onto a semantic map.
- Write paragraphs from the completed map.

Procedure

1. Explain to the student that this is a special activity to make it easier to write a story.

Figure 14
Student Map for *Stamp Collecting*

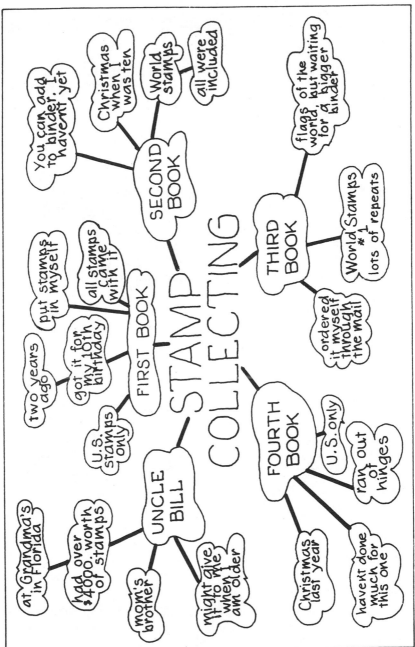

Figure 15
Student Story about *Stamp Collecting*

My Stamp Collection

I got started in stamp collecting by my great uncle Bill. He is my mom's brother. He had over $4000 worth of stamps. They are at my Grandma's house in Florida. If I'm lucky, he might give all of the stamps to me when I'm older.

The first book I got was on my tenth birthday two years ago. It was all U.S. stamps. All of the stamps came with the book, so I didn't have to buy any of them. I had to put all of the stamps in by myself after my mom taught me how.

The second book I got had world stamps in it. I got it for Christmas when I was ten years old. Like my first book, all of the stamps were included. Unlike my first book, I could add pages to this because it's a binder.

The third book also had stamps of the world. I found a lot of stamps that I already had from my second book. In this book I got world flag stamps, but I'm waiting to get a bigger binder to put them in. The most exciting thing about this book was I got to order it myself through the mail.

For Christmas last year I got another stamp book. It is very big and has only United States stamps. I haven't done much in this book because I ran out of hinges to attach the stamps to the pages in the book. I'm hoping to get some hinges for my birthday which is in two weeks, so that I can get going on this book. I really like collecting stamps.

2. Ask the student to think of a topic he is interested in and would like to write about. (The student chose to write about stamp collecting, a topic of high personal interest.)
3. Write the words *Stamp Collecting* in the center of a sheet of large paper and circle it.
4. Ask what the student knows about stamp collecting. Through discussion elicit main ideas and supporting details. Record these on the map using the main ideas as category headings and the supporting details as the information listed under the categories. Use colored pens so that each major category and its details are written in a different color. This helps the student to associate the supporting details with the main idea and facilitates paragraph writing later. (See Figure 14.)
5. Review the information on the map. Then for each major category, discuss the information listed in terms of a main idea and supporting details. Have the student rewrite the information in complete sentences. For each category, the student should first write the topic sentence of the paragraph and then the supporting sentences. Write each of the paragraphs in the color corresponding to the color used to record the information on the map. (The story the student wrote from the map *Stamp Collecting* is presented in Figure 15.)
6. Give the student an opportunity to share the map and story with other students in the language arts program.

Comments

In this example, semantic mapping was successfully combined with the language experience approach to reading and writing. This approach capitalized on the student's own interests, knowledge, and language to improve reading and writing skills. Because both the interest and the knowledge were already present, the student was able to concentrate fully on organizing the information onto a map which then served as a blueprint for paragraph writing.

Color coding played a key role in both map development and story writing. Each category (main idea) and its details were written in a different color. Each paragraph was then written in the color which corresponded with the category color. The student found the color coding system beneficial in determining the main idea and supporting details of each paragraph.

The teacher reported that after using the color coding system to write four different language experience stories, the student no longer needed colors to help map and write stories. Subsequent story mapping and writing exercises, without the use of colored pencils, proved that the student could organize, map, and write without color coding.

The semantic mapping procedure can help students organize ideas prior to writing in content area classes as well. This process gives students the opportunity to organize thoughts and information. A completed map may easily serve as a guide to structure a story or a report, with the category headings as topic sentences or main ideas for the paragraphs and the underlying details as the content.

The student who participated in this writing lesson has continued to use mapping as a prewriting strategy and as a study skill technique, indicating that he has mastered the technique and finds it a useful and effective learning tool. When this student was required to write an outline in social studies class, he first developed a semantic map and then used the map as a tool to help him create a traditional outline.

A Study Skill in English Class: Grade Eight

In this application, a modification of the Hanf semantic mapping technique is used with an English literature class of eighth graders. The students are assigned to read *The Pearl*, a novel by John Steinbeck. After all the students have read the novel, the class works together to develop a "tree like" semantic map to organize the story structure, the main ideas, and the pertinent supporting details of the story. Then each student transfers the information from the semantic map to the format of a traditional outline. (See Figures 16 and 17.)

Objectives

The semantic mapping lesson is used to meet the following objectives:
- Learn key vocabulary words from the novel.
- Identify the main ideas and supporting details of *The Pearl*.
- Improve ability to organize information.
- Develop skills in outlining.

Procedure

Day 1
1. Instruct the students to read *The Pearl* and to make a sequential list of the main events in the story.

Days 2 and 3
1. Give students time to read the novel and to record the main events.

Day 4
1. After the students have finished reading the novel and making their lists, review the general procedure for developing a semantic map. Then draw a "tree like" map on the chalkboard.

Figure 16
Completed Classroom Map for *The Pearl* by John Steinbeck

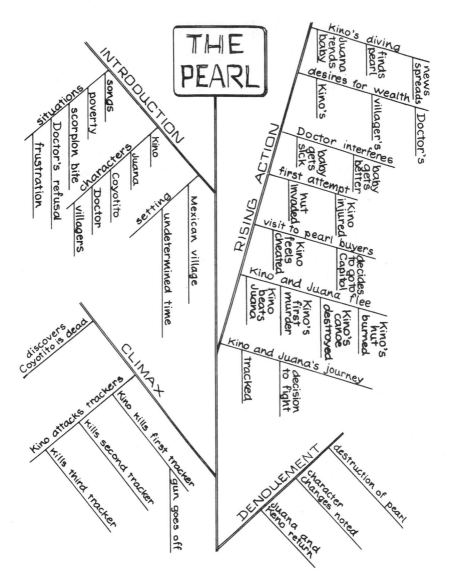

Figure 17
Traditional Outline for *The Pearl* by John Steinbeck

THE PEARL

I. INTRODUCTION
  A. Setting
    1. Mexican village
    2. undetermined time

  B. Characters
    1. Kino
    2. Juana
    3. Coyotito
    4. Doctor
    5. villagers

  C. Situations
    1. songs
    2. poverty
    3. scorpion bite
    4. Doctor's refusal to aid
    5. Kino's frustration

II. RISING ACTION
  A. Kino's diving
    1. Juana tends baby
    2. Kino finds pearl
    3. news spreads

  B. Desires for wealth
    1. Kino's
    2. villager's
    3. Doctor's

  C. Doctor interferes
    1. baby gets sick
    2. baby gets better

  D. First attempt to steal pearl
    1. hut invaded
    2. Kino injured

  E. Visit to pearl buyers
    1. Kino feels cheated
    2. Kino decides to go to Capitol

  F. Kino and Juana flee
    1. Kino beats Juana
    2. Kino's first murder
    3. Kino's canoe destroyed
    4. Kino's hut burned

  G. Kino and Juana's journey
    1. tracked by trackers
    2. decision to fight

III. CLIMAX
  A. Kino attacks trackers
    1. kills first tracker
      a. gun goes off
    2. kills second tracker
    3. kills third tracker

  B. Kino discovers Coyotito dead

IV. DENOUEMENT
  A. Kino and Juana return
  B. Character changes noted
  C. Destruction of pearl

2. Explain that the class is going to work together and put information on a map so that the completed map will display the story structure of *The Pearl*.
3. Encourage the students to refer to their lists of main events as they discuss the plot development, main ideas, and supporting details of

the story. As information is suggested, add it to the appropriate branch of the map. (See Figure 17.) During the discussion, highlight and discuss vocabulary words important to the comprehension of the novel.

Day 5
1. Review the format of a traditional outline, discuss its applications, and point out the similarities between it and the semantic map.
2. Instruct the students to work individually to transfer the information from the semantic map to the traditional outline format.
3. Give the students an opportunity to share their traditional outlines. (A sample student outline is presented in Figure 18.)
4. Again, compare and discuss the two types of organizational formats (the semantic map and the traditional outline). Ask the students to state their preferences for the use of each and to explain the reasons for their choices.
5. Direct the students to work in pairs using either the semantic map, the traditional outline, or both, to prepare for a test on the novel.

Comments

In this example, the instructional procedure of semantic mapping both enhanced story comprehension and improved students' skills in outlining. Creating the semantic map assisted the students in a variety of ways. It gave them the opportunity to lay out visually the plot of the novel. This, in itself, triggered and guided indepth discussions of the story events and also provided the students with a graphic picture of the story as a whole.

The students in this classroom had been experiencing great difficulty in developing traditional outlines in their content area classes. This teacher creatively capitalized on the opportunity to use semantic mapping to reinforce traditional outlining skills. The teacher involved the students in a simple, uncomplicated way to select and organize information. In the followup outlining activity, students were then able to transfer easily the information from the map to the more difficult format of the traditional outline. Through this activity, students were able to compare the two different outlining strategies and to understand and appreciate both.

A Study Skill in History: Grade Seven

In this application, semantic mapping is used over a period of several days with a seventh grade history class of twenty-seven high average students. Here, the mapping procedure is used both as a motivational and as an organizational tool. First, the semantic mapping procedure is used to introduce a unit on Vikings. Then the semantic map is used to record and organize information as it is presented in the unit. Finally, the completed map is used as a study tool to help the students prepare for the unit test. (See Figure 18.)

Objectives

The semantic mapping process is used to meet the following objectives:
- Assess the students' prior knowledge.
- Learn key vocabulary words related to the topic.
- Develop an organized graphic study guide.
- Self assess recall of information presented in the unit.

Procedure

Day 1
1. Write the word *Vikings* on a large sheet of paper posted on the classroom wall.
2. Ask the students to share ideas or information relating to Vikings.
3. As ideas and information are suggested, write words that relate to one another in clusters around the word *Vikings* with a black marker.
4. Ask the students to suggest labels for the clusters or categories and add them to the map. If there are areas to be studied that were not mentioned during the discussion, add these categories to the map. Tell the students that they should look for information that would fit in these categories when they later read their text and view a filmstrip about Vikings.
5. Give students art paper and direct them to copy the class map onto their individual papers. Encourage them to create a design in the center to reflect the Vikings concept. Remind them to leave room on the map so that they can add new information about Vikings.
6. Have the students read the assigned chapter in the text and then add information to their individual maps.

Day 2
1. Briefly review the category headings on the classroom map.
2. Tell the students they are going to view a filmstrip about Vikings and they should watch for information to add to their maps.
3. Show the filmstrip and give the students an opportunity to add information to their individual maps.

Day 3
1. Using the large group map, review the information about Vikings. Then have students share information they added to their own maps. Student recorders should write the new information onto the group map using a red marker.

Figure 18
Student Map for *Vikings*

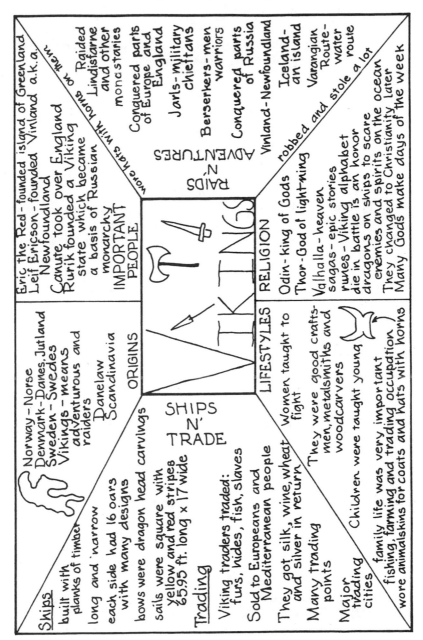

IMPORTANT PEOPLE

Eric the Red - founded island of Greenland
Leif Ericson - founded Vinland a.k.a. Newfoundland
Canute took over England
Rurik founded a Viking state which became a basis of Russian monarchy

RAIDS 'N' ADVENTURES

wore hats with horns or them
Raided Lindisfarne and other monastaries
Conquered parts of Europe and England
Jarls - military chieftains
Berserkers - men warriors
Conquered parts of Russia
Vinland - Newfoundland
Iceland - an island
Varangian Route - water route
robbed and stole a lot

RELIGION

Odin - king of Gods
Thor - God of lightning
Valhalla - heaven
sagas - epic stories
runes - Viking alphabet
die in battle is an honor
dragons on ships to scare enemies and spirits on the ocean
They changed to Christianity later
Many Gods make days of the week

LIFESTYLES

Women taught to fight
They were good craftsmen, metalsmiths and woodcarvers
Children were taught young
family life was very important
fishing, farming and trading occupation
wore animalskins for coats and hats with horns

SHIPS N' TRADE

Ships
built with planks of timber
long and narrow
each side had 16 oars
bows were dragon head carvings
sails were square with yellow and red stripes
25.95 ft. long x 17 wide

Trading
Viking traders traded: furs, hides, fish, slaves
Sold to Europeans and Mediterranean people
They got silk, wine, wheat and silver in return
Many trading points
Major trading cities

ORIGINS

Norway - Norse
Denmark - Danes, Jutland
Sweden - Swedes
Vikings - means adventurous and raiders
Danelaw
Scandinavia

VIKINGS

2. Underline and review important vocabulary words already on the map. Discuss and then add other important vocabulary words to the map and circle them.
3. Have the students add information from the large group map to their individual maps. Students should circle the vocabulary words which are either underlined or circled on the group map.

Day 4
1. Collect the students' individual maps and take down the class map from the classroom wall.
2. Post a skeletal map for *Vikings* on the classroom wall. (This map should be drawn on a large sheet of paper and should include only the title *Vikings* and the category headings that appeared on the classroom map.)
3. Tell the students to try to re-create the class map to see how much they remember about Vikings. Proceeding category by category, give the students an opportunity to add information to the map.
4. After the students have added all the information they can remember, hang up the original class map and compare it to the re-created map.
5. Return the students' individual maps and encourage students to use them to study for the upcoming test. (A copy of one student's map is shown in Figure 18.)

Comments

On the first day of the lesson, semantic mapping was used to initiate the unit of study. The technique of brainstorming prompted students to focus their thoughts on the topic of *Vikings* and to retrieve or recall information related to the topic. The initial brainstorming activity showed the students how much they already knew about the topic; the teacher reported that the students' confidence in their own knowledge base seemed to create a desire to learn more. The re-creation of the map on the fourth day of the lesson allowed students to assess how much they remembered about Vikings. They also were able to identify those areas which needed further study. The individual maps that students created served as a personal study guide for the unit.

The students were offered the opportunity of personalizing their individual maps with art paper and magic markers. Although the focus of this lesson should not be placed on designing the map itself, this proved to be an interesting motivational technique.

Student involvement in the group mapping process, both as contributors and recorders, promoted a feeling of shared ownership of the map. The teacher served as a facilitator, rather than as the director, in the map's development.

A Final Word

Semantic mapping has been found to be a useful strategy in prior knowledge activation and assessment, vocabulary building, passage comprehension, and study skill development. A major strength of the semantic mapping strategy is that it helps students to construct a model for organizing and integrating information that can then be applied to a wide variety of situations.

Semantic mapping is not only a valuable strategy to use in specific reading and content area lessons, as demonstrated in the preceding ten classroom applications, but it is also an effective way to illustrate the relationships between content areas in a major instructional unit. For example, if art or music projects were part of a social studies unit on the U.S. Civil War, a semantic mapping activity could be used to bridge the relationships of all the content related information. This map might then be displayed to demonstrate the relationships of the separate content area projects to the central idea of the whole unit—the Civil War. The map would provide a synthesized focus of the diverse classroom activities.

Semantic mapping has been used successfully by teachers with students of all grade levels, by college students, and by adults. The procedure has been found to be useful with students who are learning disabled, students in remedial reading classes, and illiterate adults. This versatile strategy can be used with large groups, small groups, pairs of students, and individuals.

Semantic mapping appears to motivate students of all age levels and to involve them actively in the thinking-reading process. Based on observations of student reaction while conducting pilot sessions using semantic mapping, Hagen (1980) suggested that the strategy may have great potential as a motivator. She reported that students involved in the mapping process showed a high level of interest. Even students initially reluctant to participate in what was, to them, a new process, contributed eagerly after a short time and continued their active involvement throughout the semantic mapping sessions.

In semantic mapping activities, the teacher is allowed to function as a facilitator. This less directive role encourages students to share in and direct their own learning. While semantic mapping affords students opportunities to draw from their prior knowledge, it is important that students verify questionable information. In this role, semantic mapping triggers further student research of a topic. The altered teacher/student relationship inherent in the semantic mapping process might explain the impact of semantic mapping as a strong motivational and brainstorming technique. The motivational characteristic of semantic mapping deserves further research to help teachers appropriately and effectively use the technique in the classroom.

The semantic mapping process facilitates text comprehension in that it draws upon and capitalizes on the categorical nature of memory. During semantic mapping, the topic (word or words) triggers the brain to retrieve information being stored in memory. When this knowledge is activated and applied to text, a link is made between past experiences and text concepts. The process of semantic mapping also allows teachers to assess and interpret what students know as well as to make judgments concerning the appropriate instruction needed. These judgments can be based upon what students demonstrate they already know about a topic, rather than teachers having to assume what the students know.

Semantic mapping should be treated as any other instructional strategy: It should be called upon and used appropriately. Because the approach can be used in so many different situations, care must be taken to ensure that it not be overused. Semantic mapping, however, needs to be taught and used in a consistent manner to enable students to reap the benefits from the process. The ultimate goal of semantic mapping instruction would be to provide students with an understanding of when to select semantic mapping as an independent reading/learning strategy and how to use it most effectively.

References

Adams, M., and Bruce, B. *Background knowledge and reading comprehension,* Reading Education Report No. 13. Urbana, IL: University of Illinois, Center for the Study of Reading, 1980.

Barrett, M.T., and Graves, M.F. A vocabulary program for junior high school remedial readers. *Journal of Reading,* 1981, *25,* 146-150.

Davis, F.B. Fundamental factor of comprehension in reading. *Psychometrika,* 1944, *9,* 185-197.

Durkin, D. What is the value of the new interest in reading comprehension? *Language Arts,* 1981, *58,* 23-41.

Hagen, J.E. *The effects of selected prereading vocabulary building activities on literal comprehension, vocabulary understanding, and attitudes of fourth and fifth grade students with reading problems.* Doctoral dissertation, University of

Wisconsin at Madison. *Dissertation Abstracts International,* 1980, *40,* 6216A. (University Microfilms No. 80-07, 553)

Hanf, M.B. Mapping: A technique for translating reading into thinking. *Journal of Reading,* 1971, *14,* 225-230, 270.

Hayes, D.A., and Tierney, R.J. Developing readers' knowledge through analogy. *Reading Research Quarterly,* 1982, *17,* 256-280.

Johnson, D.D., and Pearson, P.D. *Teaching reading vocabulary,* second edition. New York: Holt, Rinehart and Winston, 1984.

Johnson, D.D., Pittelman, S.D., Toms-Bronowski, S., and Levin, K.M. *An investigation of the effects of prior knowledge and vocabulary acquisition on passage comprehension,* Program Report 84-5. Madison, WI: Wisconsin Center for Education Research, University of Wisconsin, 1984.

Johnson, D.D., Toms-Bronowski, S., and Pittelman, S.D. *An investigation of the effectiveness of semantic mapping and semantic feature analysis with intermediate grade level students,* Program Report 83-3. Madison, WI: Wisconsin Center for Education Research, University of Wisconsin, 1982.

Johnston, P. Background knowledge and reading comprehension test bias. *Reading Research Quarterly,* 1984, *19,* 219-239.

Johnston, P., and Pearson, P.D. *Prior knowledge connectivity and the assessment of reading comprehension,* Technical Report No. 245. Urbana, IL: University of Illinois, 1982.

Jones, S.T. *The effects of semantic mapping on vocabulary acquisition and reading comprehension of black innercity students.* Unpublished doctoral dissertation, University of Wisconsin at Madison, 1984. (University Microfilms No. 84-17, 954)

Karbon, J.C. *An investigation of the relationships between prior knowledge and vocabulary development using semantic mapping with culturally diverse students.* Unpublished doctoral dissertation, University of Wisconsin at Madison, 1984.

Margosein, C.M., Pascarella, E.T., and Pflaum, S.W. *The effects of instruction using semantic mapping on vocabulary and comprehension.* Paper presented at the Annual Meeting of the American Educational Research Association, New York, 1982. (ED 217 390)

National Institute of Education. *Conference on studies in reading.* Washington, D.C.: U.S. Department of Health, Education and Welfare, 1978.

Pearson, P.D. Changing the face of reading comprehension instruction. *The Reading Teacher,* 1985, *38,* 724-737.

Pearson, P.D., and Johnson, D.D. *Teaching reading comprehension.* New York: Holt, Rinehart and Winston, 1978.

Pearson, P.D., and Spiro, R. The new buzz word in reading is schema. *Instructor,* 1982, *91,* 46-48.

Pittelman, S.D., Levin, K.M., and Johnson, D.D. *An investigation of two instructional settings in the use of semantic mapping with poor readers,* Program Report 85-4. Madison, WI: Wisconsin Center for Education Research, University of Wisconsin, 1985.

Spearritt, D. Identification of subskills of reading comprehension by maximum likelihood factor analysis. *Reading Research Quarterly,* 1972, *8,* 92-111.

Thorndike, R.L. *Reading as reasoning.* Paper presented to Division 15, American Psychological Association, Washington, DC, 1971.

Toms-Bronowski, S. *An investigation of the effectiveness of selected vocabulary teaching strategies with intermediate grade level students.* Doctoral dissertation, University of Wisconsin at Madison. *Dissertation Abstracts International,* 1983, *44,* 1405A. (University Microfilms No. 83-16, 238)

Suggested Readings on Semantic Mapping

Baumann, J.F., and Johnson, D.D. *Reading instruction and the beginning teacher.* Minneapolis, MN: Burgess, 1984.

Cleland, C.J. Highlighting issues in children's literature through semantic webbing. *The Reading Teacher,* 1981, *34,* 642-646.

Freedman, G., and Reynolds, E.G. Enriching basal reader lessons with semantic webbing. *The Reading Teacher,* 1980, *33,* 677-684.

Hanf, M.B. Mapping: A technique for translating reading into thinking. *Journal of Reading,* 1971, *14,* 225-230, 270.

Johnson, D.D. *Three sound strategies for vocabulary development.* Ginn Occasional Paper Number 3. Lexington, MA: Ginn, 1981.

Johnson, D.D., and Pearson, P.D. *Teaching reading vocabulary,* second edition. New York: Holt, Rinehart and Winston, 1984.

McNeil, J.D. *Reading comprehension: New directions for classroom practice.* Glenview, IL: Scott, Foresman, 1984.

Pearson, P.D., and Johnson, D.D. *Teaching reading comprehension.* New York: Holt, Rinehart and Winston, 1978.

Sinatra, R.C., Berg, D., and Dunn, R. Semantic mapping improves reading comprehension of learning disabled students. *Teaching Exceptional Children,* 1985, *17,* 310-314.